قَالَ اللهُ تَعَالَى:

وَرَتِّلِ الْقُرْآنَ تَرْتِيلًا

اَلْحَمْدُ لِلّٰهِ عَلَى اِحْسَانِهِ وَاِنْعَامِهِ

TAJWEED

FOR

BEGINNERS

By
M.Q.I. ISHAQ

Islamic Book Service (P) Ltd.
New Delhi

TAJWEED FOR BEGINNERS

Author
M.Q.I. Ishaq

ISBN 978-81-7231-467-5

First Published 2003
Twelfth Impression 2014
Revised Edition 2016
Fifth Impression 2020

Published by *Abdus Sami* for :

Islamic Book Service (P) Ltd.

1516-18, Pataudi House, Darya Ganj, New Delhi-110002 (India)
Tel.: +91-11-23244556, 23253514, 23269050, 23286551
e-mail: info@ibsbookstore.com
Website: www.ibsbookstore.com
amazon.in: www.bit.do/ibs

OUR ASSOCIATES
Husami Book Depot, Hyderabad (India)

Printed in India

CONTENTS

THE IMPORTANCE OF
TAJWEED

Allah Ta'ala states in the Quraan Majeed:

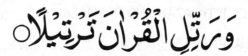

"And recite the Quraan with measure."

In the commentary of this verse, Hazrat Ali (Radhiallaho 'Anh) states:

"Tarteel means to know the Tajweed of the letters and to recognize the places of pausing."

In another place, Allah Ta'ala says:

"And with measure have we revealed it (the Quraan)."

In a Hadith it has been narrated:

"Allah desires that the Quraan be recited in the manner it was revealed."

Since the Quraan was revealed with **Tajweed**, it is compulsory to recite the Quraan with **Tajweed**. We also know that Allah Ta'ala has made it compulsory upon us to learn **Tajweed** because without the knowledge of **Tajweed**, we will not be able to recite the Quraan with Tajweed. If we do not do so, then we are liable to be sinful especially those that do not care, for it is narrated that many are they who recite the Quraan, while the Quraan curses them.

TAJWEED

TAJWEED MEANS: To recite every letter CORRECTLY, from it's Makhraj, with all it's Qualities.

THE PURPOSE OF TAJWEED: To recite the QURAAN in the manner IT was revealed to, AND recited by NABI-E-KAREEM SALLALLAHU 'ALAIHI WASALLAM.

THE BENEFIT OF LEARNING AND RECITING THE QURAAN, WITH TAJWEED is that a person will be honoured in this world (DUNYA) and the Hereafter (AAKHIRAT).

NOTE: It is COMPULSORY (FARDH) to learn TAJWEED.

QUESTIONS

1. What is the definition of Tajweed?

2. What is the purpose and benefit of Tajweed?

3. What is the law (rule) concerning Tajweed?

5

ERRORS

Errors which are made whilst reciting the QURAAN are of TWO TYPES:

1. MAJOR ERRORS   ا لَحْنِ جَلِى

2. MINOR ERRORS   ٢ لَحْنِ خَفِى

1. MAJOR ERRORS

1. To recite one letter in place of another;

e.g. instead of reciting اَلْحَمْدُ a person recites اَلْحَنْدُ or instead of ث a person recites س or in place of ط he recites ت and so on.

2. To add a letter to a word

e.g. a person adds a و after the د in and اَلْحَمْدُ a ى after لِلّٰه thus reciting اَلْحَمْدُوْلِلّٰهِىْ

3. To delete a letter from a word

e.g. not to recite the و in لَمْ يُوْلَدْ and thus recite it as لَمْ يُلَدْ

4. To recite one HARKAT in place of another

e.g. to recite with a KASRAH (ZER) on the ك in اِيَّاكَ instead of a FATHAH (ZABAR) or to recite the HAMZAH in اِهْدِنَا with a FATHAH instead of KASRAH.

5. To recite a HARKAT in place of a JAZM

e.g. To read on both the ن and/or م with a ZABAR thus اَنْعَمْتَ

NOTE: To make any of the above mentioned errors is a MAJOR SIN AND HARAAM. It is COMPULSORY TO REFRAIN FROM THESE ERRORS.

2. MINOR ERRORS:

Those errors (mistakes) a person makes, when he does not

recite with any of those RULES which show the BEAUTY OF THE QURAAN-E-KAREEM

e.g. not to recite the ر in صِرَاطٍ with a full mouth when it has a FAT<u>H</u>AH or not to recite the TWO ل in الله with a full mouth when there is a FAT<u>H</u>AH or a DHAMMAH (pesh) before them, or not to make GHUNNAH, IKHFAA or MADD.

NOTE: To make any of these Minor Errors is a MINOR SIN AND MAKROOH. To refrain from these errors is also NECESSARY.

QUESTIONS

1. Give the names of the two types of errors?

2. Name any three Major Errors?

3. What is the Law (rule) concerning Major and Minor Errors?

4. What are Minor Errors?

THE RULES OF ISTI'AAZAH اِسْتِعَاذَةٌ
AND BASMALAH بَسْمَلَةٌ

Before reciting the QURAAN-E-KAREEM, it is NECESSARY to recite ISTI'AAZAH.

أَعُوْذُبِاللهِ مِنَ الشَّيْطٰنِ الرَّجِيْمِ

When STARTING a SURAH, it will be NECESSARY to recite BASMALAH

بِسْمِ اللهِ الرَّحْمٰنِ الرَّحِيْمِ

BUT NOT AT THE BEGINNING OF SURAH TAUBAH (PARAH 10)

If commencing anywhere in a SURAH, besides the beginning, then it will be OPTIONAL to recite BASMALAH, but it will be BETTER IF RECITED.

Whilst reciting the QURAAN-E-KAREEM, if a person speaks of worldly affairs, OR replies to someone's SALAAM, OR has something to eat or drink, then it will be NECESSARY for him to REPEAT THE ISTI'AAZAH BEFORE CONTINUING.

A. THE RECITATION OF ISTI'AAZAH AND BASMALAH THE BEGINNING OF A SURAH.

This can be done in Four ways:

1. WASLE KUL.   وَصْلِ كُلْ
2. WASLE AWWAL- FASLE THANI.   وَصْلِ اَوَّلْ فَصْلِ ثَانِيْ
3. FASLE AWWAL- WASLE THANI.   فَصْلِ اَوَّلْ وَصْلِ ثَانِيْ
4. FASLE KUL.   فَصْلِ كُلْ

NOTE: WASL means: To recite TOGETHER.

FASL means: To recite SEPARATELY.

Therefore;

1. WASLE KUL means to recite ALL together.
2. WASLE AWWAL - FASLE THANI means to recite the FIRST TWO together and the THIRD separately.

3. **FASLE AWWAL - WASLE THANI** means to recite the FIRST separately and join the SECOND AND THIRD.

4. **FASLE KUL** means to recite ALL separately.

1. **WASLE KUL:** To recite ISTI'AAZAH AND BASMALAH and the beginning of the SURAH together.

e.g. أَعُوْذُ بِاللّٰهِ مِنَ الشَّيْطٰنِ الرَّجِيْمِ ۙ بِسْمِ اللّٰهِ الرَّحْمٰنِ الرَّحِيْمِ ۙ

اَلْحَمْدُ لِلّٰهِ رَبِّ الْعٰلَمِيْنَ ۞

2. **WASLE AWWAL - FASLE THANI:** To recite ISTI'AAZAH AND BASMALAH together, stopping after BASMALAH and reciting the beginning of the Surah separately.

e.g. أَعُوْذُ بِاللّٰهِ مِنَ الشَّيْطٰنِ الرَّجِيْمِ ۙ بِسْمِ اللّٰهِ الرَّحْمٰنِ الرَّحِيْمِ ۙ

اَلْحَمْدُ لِلّٰهِ رَبِّ الْعٰلَمِيْنَ ۞

3. **FASLE AWWAL - WASLE THANI:** To recite ISTI'AAZAH separately and BASMALAH and the beginning of the surah together.

e.g. أَعُوْذُ بِاللّٰهِ مِنَ الشَّيْطٰنِ الرَّجِيْمِ ۙ بِسْمِ اللّٰهِ الرَّحْمٰنِ الرَّحِيْمِ ۙ

اَلْحَمْدُ لِلّٰهِ رَبِّ الْعٰلَمِيْنَ ۞

4. **FASLE KUL:** To recite ISTI'AAZAH, BASMALAH and the beginning of the surah separately.

e.g. أَعُوْذُ بِاللّٰهِ مِنَ الشَّيْطٰنِ الرَّجِيْمِ ۙ بِسْمِ اللّٰهِ الرَّحْمٰنِ الرَّحِيْمِ ۙ

اَلْحَمْدُ لِلّٰهِ رَبِّ الْعٰلَمِيْنَ ۞

B. THE RECITING OF ISTI'AAZAH, BASMALAH AND ANYWHERE IN BETWEEN A SURAH, BESIDES THE BEGINNING COULD BE DONE IN FOUR WAYS.

NOTE: Only Two ways are permissible, i.e. FASLE KUL AND WASLE AWWAL - FASLE THANI. The remaining TWO ways are NOT permissible.

1. **FASLE KUL:** To recite ISTI'AAZAH BASMALAH and the AAYAT all separately. To recite in this way is permissible.

اَعُوْذُ بِاللّٰهِ مِنَ الشَّيْطٰنِ الرَّجِيْمِ ۘ بِسْمِ اللّٰهِ الرَّحْمٰنِ الرَّحِيْمِ ۘ .e.g

اِنَّ لِلْمُتَّقِيْنَ مَفَازًا۠ا

2. **WASLE AWWAL - FASLE THANI:** To recite ISTI'AAZAH and BASMALAH together and the AAYAT SEPARATELY. To recite in this way is permissible

اَعُوْذُ بِاللّٰهِ مِنَ الشَّيْطٰنِ الرَّجِيْمِ ۘ بِسْمِ اللّٰهِ الرَّحْمٰنِ الرَّحِيْمِ ۘ .e.g

اِنَّ لِلْمُتَّقِيْنَ مَفَازًا۠ا

3. **FASLE AWWAL - WASLE THANI:** To recite ISTI'AAZAH separately, and BASMALAH and the AAYAT together. To recite in this way is NOT permissible.

اَعُوْذُ بِاللّٰهِ مِنَ الشَّيْطٰنِ الرَّجِيْمِ ۘ بِسْمِ اللّٰهِ الرَّحْمٰنِ الرَّحِيْمِ ۘ .e.g

اِنَّ لِلْمُتَّقِيْنَ مَفَازًا۠ا

4. **WASLE KUL:** To recite ISTI'AAZAH BASMALAH and the AAYAT together. To recite in this way is NOT permissible

اَعُوْذُ بِاللّٰهِ مِنَ الشَّيْطٰنِ الرَّجِيْمِ ۘ بِسْمِ اللّٰهِ الرَّحْمٰنِ الرَّحِيْمِ ۘ .e.g

اِنَّ لِلْمُتَّقِيْنَ مَفَازًا۠ا

C. THE COMPLETING OF A SURAH AND THE BEGINNING OF THE NEXT SURAH COULD BE DONE IN FOUR WAYS.

1. **WASLE KUL:** To recite the END of a SURAH BASMALAH and the BEGINNING of the NEXT SURAH all together.

وَاَمَّا بِنِعْمَةِ رَبِّكَ فَحَدِّثْ۠ بِسْمِ اللّٰهِ الرَّحْمٰنِ الرَّحِيْمِ ۘ .e.g

اَلَمْ نَشْرَحْ لَكَ صَدْرَكَ۠

2. **WASLE AWWAL - FASLE THANI:** To recite the END of a SURAH and BASMALAH together and the beginning of the NEXT SURAH separately.

وَاَمَّا بِنِعْمَةِ رَبِّكَ فَحَدِّثْ۠ بِسْمِ اللّٰهِ الرَّحْمٰنِ الرَّحِيْمِ ۘ .e.g

اَلَمْ نَشْرَحْ لَكَ صَدْرَكَ۠

NOTE: To recite in this manner is NOT permissible, as a person may think that BASMALAH is part of the PREVIOUS SURAH, whereas the place of BASMALAH is at the beginning of the SURAH, not the end.

3. **FASLE AWWAL - WASLE THANI:** To recite THE END of a SURAH separately, and BASMALAH and the BEGINNING or the NEXT SURAH together

   e.g.   وَاَمَّا بِنِعْمَةِ رَبِّكَ فَحَدِّثْ۞   بِسْمِ اللهِ الرَّحْمٰنِ الرَّحِيْمِ ۬
   اَلَمْ نَشْرَحْ لَكَ صَدْرَكَ۞

4. **FASLE KUL:** To recite the END of A SURAH BASMALAH and the BEGINNING of the NEXT SURAH separately.

   e.g.   وَاَمَّا بِنِعْمَةِ رَبِّكَ فَحَدِّثْ۞   بِسْمِ اللهِ الرَّحْمٰنِ الرَّحِيْمِ ۬
   اَلَمْ نَشْرَحْ لَكَ صَدْرَكَ۞

QUESTIONS

1. What does the terms ISTI'AAZAH and BASMALAH mean?
2. When should ISTI'AAZAH be read?
3. When will BASMALAH be read?
4. When will it be necessary to repeat the ISTI'AAZAH?
5. What does wasl and Fasl mean?
6. When starting a surat, in how many ways could ISTI'AAZAH BASMALAH and the beginning of the surat be read?
7. Will it be permissible to recite Wasle Awwal-Fasle Thani when completing one surah and beginning the next? Give the reason also.

Hadhrat 'Uthman RA narrates that Rasulullah (Salallahu-'Alaihi-Wasallam) said:

"The best amongst you is he who learns the Quraan and teaches it."

If there was no Hadith except this Hadith it would have been sufficient to prove the importance and virtue of the Holy Quraan.

THE ARABIC ALPHABET ARE 29 WHICH ARE AS FOLLOWS:

ج جِيۡمۡ	ث ثَا	ت تَا	ب بَا	ا اَلِف
JEEM	THAA	TAA	BAA	ALIF
ر رَا	ذ ذَاۡل	د دَاۡل	خ خَا	ح حَا
RAA	ZAAL	DALL	KHAA	HAA
ض ضَاۡد	ص صَاۡد	ش شِيۡن	س سِيۡن	ز زَا
DHAAD	SAAD	SHEEN	SEEN	ZAA
ف فَا	غ غَيۡن	ع عَيۡن	ظ ظَا	ط طَا
FAA	GHAIN	'AIN	ZHAA	TAA
ن نُوۡن	م مِيۡمۡ	ل لَاۡمۡ	ك كَاۡف	ق قَاۡف
NOON	MEEM	LAAM	KAAF	QAAF

ى يَا	ء هَمۡزَهۡ	ه هَا	و وَآوۡ
YAA	HAMZAH	HAA	WAAW

MAKHAARIJ

Makhraj is the place where the sound of the letter originates.

According to Imaam Khalif Rahmatullahi-alaih there are 17 MAKHAARIJ.

1. JOWFE-FAM جَوْفِ فَمْ .

Emptiness of the mouth.

From this Makhraj is pronounced the three letters of

MADD ا و ى

e.g. نُوْحِيْهَا .

They are known as HUROOFE-MADDAH حُرُوْفِ مَدَّه and HUROOFE-HAWA-IEYAH حُرُوْفِ هَوَائِيَّه .

2. AQSA-E-HALQ أَقْصٰى حَلْق .

The part of the throat nearest to the chest.

From this Makhraj is pronounced the letter ء and ه .

3. WASTE-HALQ وَسْطِ حَلْق .

The centre of the throat.

From this Makhraj is pronounced the letters ع and ح .

4. ADNAA-E-HALQ أَدْنٰى حَلْق .

The part of the throat nearest to the mouth.

From this Makhraj is pronounced the letters غ and خ .

NOTE: The above letters خ غ ح ع ه ء are known as HUROOFE-HALQI حُرُوْفِ حَلْقِى as they originate from the throat.

5. THE EXTREME BACK OF THE TONGUE WHEN TOUCHING THE PALATE.

From this Makhraj the letter ق is pronounced.

6. THE BACK OF THE TONGUE, (BUT NOT AS FAR BACK AS THAT OF QAAF, A LITTLE TO THE FRONT OF THE MOUTH) WHEN TOUCHING THE PALATE.

From this Makhraj the letter ك is pronounced

NOTE: The letters ق and ك are known as

HUROOFE-LAHATIYAH حُرُوْفِ لَهَاتِيَّہ and HUROOFE-LAHWIYAH حُرُوْفِ لَهْوِيَّہ because the are pronounced from near the LAHAAT لَهَاتُ Uvula

7. THE CENTRE OF THE TONGUE WHEN TOUCHING THE PALATE.

From this Makhraj is pronounced the letters ج ش ى GHAIR MADDAH.

NOTE: The letters ج ش ى GHAIR MADDAH are Known as HUROOFE-SHAJRIYAH حُرُوْفِ شَجْرِيَّہ because they are pronounced from the centre of the mouth.

THE TEETH

A person commonly has 32 teeth. They are as follows:

THANAYA: ثَنَايَا Central Incisors (4)

Two THANAYA 'ULYA ثَنَايَاعُلْيَا Upper Central Incisors.

Two THANAYA SUFLA ثَنَايَاسُفْلیٰ Lower Central Incisors

NEXT TO THE THANAYA ON EACH SIDE ARE THE

RABA'I: رَبَاعِیٰ Lateral Incisors (4)

Two RABA'I 'ULYA رَبَاعِیٰ عُلْیَا Upper Lateral Incisors.

Two RABA'I SUFLA رَبَاعِیٰ سُفْلیٰ Lower Lateral Incisors.

NEXT TO THE RABA'I ON EACH SIDE ARE THE

ANYAAB: اَنْیَاب Canines (4)

Two ANYAAB-E-'ULYA اَنْیَاب عُلْیَا -Upper Canines.

Two ANYAAB-E-SUFLA اَنْیَاب سُفْلیٰ -Lower Canines.

NEXT TO THE ANYAAB ON EACH SIDE ARE THE

DHAWAAHIK: ضَوَاحِك First premolars (4)

Two DHAWAAHIK-E-'ULYA ضَوَاحِك عُلْیَا Upper first premolars

Two DHAWAAHIK-E-SUFLA ضَوَاحِك سُفْلیٰ Lower first premolars

NEXT TO THE DHAWAAHIK ON EACH SIDE ARE THE

TAWAAHIN طَوَاحِن Second Premolars (4).

First Molars (4),   Second Molars (4)

Six TAWAAHIN-E-'ULYA طَوَاحِن عُلْیَا

- Upper Second premolars First and Second Molars. Six
TAWAAHIN-E-SUFLA طَوَاحِن سُفْلیٰ

15

- Lower Second premolars First and Second Molars. The last tooth in the mouth on each side is called the NAWAAJI<u>Z</u>

Two Nawaaji<u>z</u> 'Ulya   نَوَاجِنُ عُلْيَا   on left and right.

Two Nawaaji<u>z</u> Sufla   نَوَاجِنُ سُفْلٰى   on left and right.

NOTE: The DHAWAA<u>H</u>IK, <u>T</u>AWAA<u>H</u>IN, NAWAAJI<u>Z</u>, TOGETHER ARE KNOWN AS THE ADHRAAS.

They are the premolars which are (8):

2	Top right	2	Top Left
2	Bottom right	2	Bottom Left

and the molars which are (12)

3	Top right	3	Top Left
3	Bottom right	3	Bottom Left.

THE TEETH

THE TEETH COMPLETE ARE 30 AND 2

THANAYA ARE 4 AND RABA'I ARE 2, 2

ANYAAB ARE 4 AND THEN 20 REMAIN

ADRAAS HAVE THE QARIS GIVEN IT'S NAME

DHAWAA<u>H</u>IK 4 AND <u>T</u>AWAA<u>H</u>IN 12 YOU KNOW

NAWAAJI<u>Z</u> SIDE BY SIDE HAS 2, 2 ALSO.

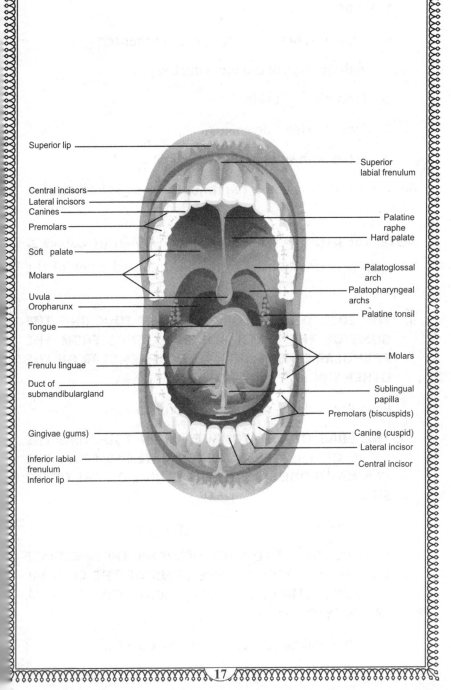

Superior lip

Superior labial frenulum

Central incisors

Lateral incisors

Canines

Premolars

Soft palate

Molars

Palatine raphe

Hard palate

Palatoglossal arch

Palatopharyngeal archs

Uvula

Oropharunx

Palatine tonsil

Tongue

Frenulu linguae

Molars

Duct of submandibulargland

Sublingual papilla

Premolars (biscuspids)

Gingivae (gums)

Canine (cuspid)

Lateral incisor

Inferior labial frenulum

Central incisor

Inferior lip

8. **THE BACK EDGE OF THE TONGUE UPTURNED WHEN TOUCHING THE ROOTS OF THE MOLARS AND THE PRE-MOLARS**

From this Makhraj the letter ض is pronounced

There are three ways of pronouncing the ض :

1. From the right side

2. From the left side

3. From both sides at the same time

But it is commonly easier to pronounce the ض from the left side

NOTE: The letter ض is known as <u>H</u>ARFE-'AAFIYAH حَرْفِ عَافِيَة because it is pronounced from the upturned sides of the tongue.

9. **THE EDGE OF THE TONGUE, WHEN TOUCHING THE GUMS OF THE TEETH, WHICH EXTENDS FROM THE PREMOLAR ON ONE SIDE, TO THE PREMOLAR ON THE OTHER SIDE.**

From this Makhraj the letter ل is pronounced.

10. **THE EDGE OF THE TONGUE, WHEN TOUCHING THE GUMS OF THE TEETH, WHICH EXTENDS FROM THE CANINE ON ONE SIDE, TO THE CANINE ON THE OTHER SIDE**

From this Makhraj the letter ن is pronounced.

11. **THE EDGE OF THE TONGUE, INCLUDING THE IMMEDIATE TOP, WHEN TOUCHING THE GUMS OF THE CENTRAL INCISORS (THANAYA 'ULYA) AND THE LATERAL INCISORS (RABA'IYAH)**

From this Makhraj the letter ر is pronounced.

NOTE: The letters ل ن ر are known as <u>H</u>UROOFE-<u>T</u>ARFIYAH حُرُوْفِ طَرْفِيَة AND <u>H</u>UROOFE-<u>Z</u>ALQIYAH حُرُوْفِ ذَلْقِيَة because they are pronounced from the edge of the tongue.

12. THE TIP OF THE TONGUE WHEN TOUCHING THE ROOTS OF THE THANAYA 'ULYA.

From this Makhraj the letters ت د ط are pronounced.

NOTE: The letters ت د ط are known as <u>H</u>UROOFE-NI<u>T</u>'IYAH حُرُوْفِ نِطْعِيَّة because they are pronounced from the cavity of the roots of the THANAYA 'ULYA

13. THE TIP OF THE TONGUE WHEN TOUCHING THE EDGE OF THE CENTRAL INCISORS (THANAYA 'ULYA)

From this Makhraj the letters ث ذ ظ are pronounced

NOTE: The letters ث ذ ظ are known as <u>H</u>UROOFE-LITHWIYAH حُرُوْفِ لِثْوِيَّة because they are pronounced from the teeth which are attached to the gums which in turn are known as LITH-THA لِثَّ

14. THE TIP OF THE TONGUE WHEN TOUCHING THE EDGE OF THE LOWER CENTRAL INCISORS (THANAYA SUFLA) INCLUDING THE UPPER CENTRAL INCISORS (THANAYA 'ULYA)

From this Makhraj the letters ز س ص are pronounced

NOTE: The letters ز س ص are known as <u>H</u>UROOFE-ASALIYAH حُرُوْفِ أَسْلِيَة because they are pronounced from the sharp tip of the tongue

15. THE INNER CENTRE OF THE BOTTOM LIP WHEN TOUCHING THE EDGE OF THE UPPER CENTRAL INCISORS (THANAYA 'ULYA).

From this Makhraj the letter ف is pronounced.

16. BOTH THE LIPS (WHEN MEETING)

From this Makhraj the letters ومرب GHAIR MADDAH are pronounced.

NOTE: 1. ب is pronounced from the wet portions of the lips.

مـ is pronounced from the dry portions of the lips.

و is pronounced by the incomplete meeting of the lips.

2. The Letters و مـ ب ف are known as <u>HUROOFE-SHAFAWIYAH</u> حُرُوْفِ شَفَوِيَّة because they are pronounced from the lips.

17. KHAISHOOM خِيْشُوْم THE NOSTRILS.

From this Makhraj the GHUNNAH is pronounced

QUESTIONS

1. Define Makhraj.

2. How many Makharij are there?

3. a. What is the Makhraj of ghair Maddah?

   b. Explain ghair Maddah.

4. Recite the poem regarding the teeth.

5. a. Which letter is known as <u>H</u>arfe 'Aafiyah?

   b. And what is it's Makhraj?

   c. How many ways are there of Pronouncing this letter?

6. Which letters are known as <u>H</u>uroofe Nit'iyah?

7. a. What is the Makhraj of the <u>H</u>uroofe Shafawiyah?

   b. Describe the difference in the Makhraj of

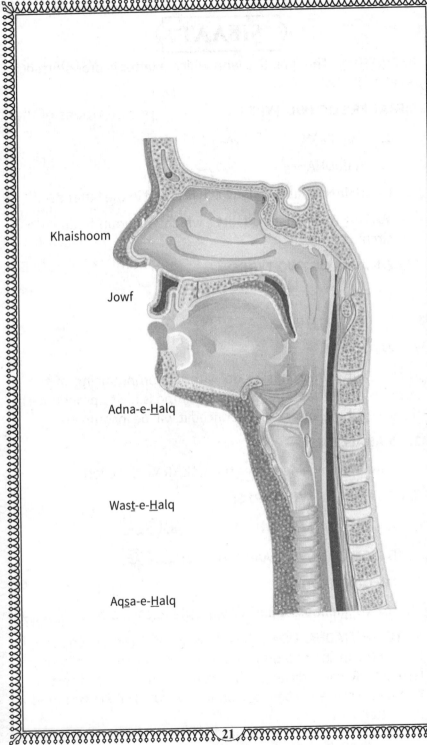

Khaishoom

Jowf

Adna-e-<u>H</u>alq

Wa<u>st</u>-e-<u>H</u>alq

Aq<u>s</u>a-e-<u>H</u>alq

21

SIFAAT

DEFINITION: The qualities with which a letter is pronounced is called SIFAAT.

SIFAAT ARE OF TWO TYPES:

1. LAAZIMAH لَازِمَة .
2. 'AARIDHAH عَارِضَة .

1. LAAZIMAH: That quality which is found in the letter itself.

2. 'AARIDHAH: That quality which is found due to circumstances.

LAAZIMAH IS OF TWO TYPES:

1. ZAATIYAH ذَاتِيَة .
2. MAHALLIYAH مَحَلِّيَة .

1. ZAATIYAH:

That quality which has to do with the pronouncing of the letter itself. Without the quality it is impossible to pronounce the letter. If the letter is pronounced it will be incomplete.

2. MAHALLIYAH:

That quality which describes the MAKHRAJ of the letter.

ZAATIYAH IS OF TWO TYPES:

A. MUTADHAADDAH مُتَضَادَّة .
B. GHAIR MUTADHAADDAH غَيْر مُتَضَادَّة .

A. MUTADHAADDAH:

Those two qualities which are opposite to each other.

NOTE: MUTADHAADDAH has five pairs. From each pair, NEITHER can the two qualities be found together in any one letter, NOR can any letter be without any one of the two qualities. From each pair, one quality will DEFINITELY be found in a letter.

B. GHAIR MUTADHAADDAH: Those qualities which have NO OPPOSITES.

A. THERE ARE TEN TYPES OF MUTADHAADDAH:

1. HAMS هَمْس (1st pair) 2. JAHR جَهْر

3. SHIDDAT شِدَّتْ (2ND PAIR) 4. RIKHWAT رِخْوَتْ

5. ISTI'LA اِسْتِعْلَاءِ (3rd pair) 6. ISTIFAAL اِسْتِفَالْ

7. ITBAAQ اِطْبَاقْ (4th pair) 8. INFITAAH اِنْفِتَاحْ

9. IZLAAQ اِذْلَاقْ (5THPAIR) 10. ISMAAT اِصْمَاتْ

1. **HAMS** هَمْس is that quality, which when pronounced, the VOICE of the letter ends off so LOW in the MAKHRAJ, that the BREATH will REMAIN FLOWING.

e.g. The ث in يَلْهَثْ.

NOTE: There are 10 LETTERS OF HAMS which are;

فَحَثَّهُ شَخْصٌ سَكَتْ

2. The LETTERS of HAMS are known as MAHMOOSAH.

3. The OPPOSITE of HAMS is JAHR.

2. **JAHR** جَهْر is that quality, which when pronounced, the VOICE of the letter ends off so HIGH in the Makhraj, that THE BREATH will not continue to flow.

e.g. The ء in مَأْكُوْلٍ.

NOTE: 1. The LETTERS of JAHR are known as MAJHOORAH مَجْهُوْرَة.

2. Besides the LETTERS of MAHMOOSAH, the rest are MAJHOORAH.

3. **SHIDDAT** شِدَّتْ is that quality, which when pronounced the VOICE of the letter will be HARD and the VOICE of the letter will END OFF in the Makhraj.

e.g. The د in اَحَدٌ.

NOTE: 1. There are 8 LETTERS of SHIDDAT, which are; اَجِدُ قَطٍ بَكَتْ.

2. The LETTERS of SHIDDAT are known as SHADEEDAH شَدِيْدَه.

3. The OPPOSITE of SHIDDAT is RIKHWAT رِخْوَتْ.

4. RIKHWAT رِخْوَتْ is that quality, which when pronounced the VOICE of the letter will be SOFT and the VOICE of the letter will REMAIN FLOWING in the MAKHRAJ.

e.g. The ش in مَعَايِشَ.

NOTE: 1. THE LETTERS of RIKHWAT are known as RIKHWAH رِخْوَه.

2. BETWEEN the QUALITIES of SHIDDAT and RIKHWAT, there is ANOTHER QUALITY known as TAWASSUT تَوَسُّط.

TAWASSUT تَوَسُّط is that quality, which when pronounced the VOICE of the letter will be BETWEEN THE QUALITY of SHIDDAT AND RIKHWAT

e.g. The ل in قُلْ.

NOTE: 1. There are five LETTERS OF TAWASSUT, which are لِنْ عُمَرُ.

2. The LETTERS of TAWASSUT are known as MUTAWASSITA مُتَوَسِّط.

3. Besides the LETTERS of SHADIDAH, AND

MUTAWASSI<u>TA</u> the REST are the LETTERS of RIKHWAT.

5. **ISTI'LA** اِسْتِعْلَاء is that quality, which when pronounced, the MAJOR PORTION of the TONGUE from the BACK, will rise towards the palate

   e.g. The خ in تَخْفِيفُ خَيْرٌ.

NOTE: 1. There are seven LETTERS of ISTI'LA which are خُصَّ ضَغْطٍ قِظْ.

2. The LETTERS of ISTI'LA are known as MUSTA'LIYAH مُسْتَعْلِيَةُ.

3. The OPPOSITE of ISTI'LA is ISTIFAAL.

6. **ISTIFAAL** اِسْتِفَالُ is that quality, which when pronounced the MAJOR PORTION of THE TONGUE, from the BACK will NOT rise towards the palate.

   e.g. The ذ in كَذَالِكَ

NOTE: 1. The LETTER of ISTIFAAL are known as MUSTAFILAH مُسْتَفِلَةُ.

2. Besides the LETTERS of MUSTA'LIYAH the REST are the LETTERS of MUSTAFILAH.

7. **ITBAAQ** اِطْبَاقٌ is that quality, which when pronounced, the CENTRE of the TONGUE WILL MEET and EMBRACE the palate.

   e.g. The ط in مَطْلَعِ الْفَجْرِ.

NOTE: 1. There are four LETTERS of I<u>T</u>BAAQ, which are ص ض ط ظ.

2. The LETTERS of I<u>T</u>BAAQ are known as MU<u>T</u>BIQAH مُطْبِقَةُ.

3. The OPPOSITE of ITBAAH is INFITAAH.

8. **INFITAAH** اِنْفِتَاخْ is that quality which when pronounced the CENTRE of the TONGUE WILL NOT MEET and COVER the palate.

   e.g. The ك in كَمُ .

NOTE: 1. The LETTERS of INFITAAH are known as MUNFATIHAH مُنْفَتِحَة .

2. Besides the LETTERS of MUTBIQAH, the REST are the LETTERS of MUNFATIHAH.

9. **IZLAAQ** اِذْلَاقُ is that quality which when pronounced, THE LETTERS, IN THEIR MAKHRAJ, are pronounced QUICKLY and SWIFTLY.

   e.g. The م in عَلَيْهِمْ .

NOTE: 1. There are six LETTERS of IZLAAQ which are فَرَّ مِنْ لُبٍّ .

2. The LETTERS of IZLAAQ are known as MUZLIQAH مُنْلِقَة .

3. The OPPOSITE of IZLAAQ is ISMAAT

10. **ISMAAT** اِصْمَاتْ is that quality which when pronounced the LETTERS IN THEIR MAKHRAJ are pronounced SLOWLY AND FIRMLY.

    e.g. The ض in وَلَاالضَّآلِّيْنَ .

NOTE: 1. The LETTERS of ISMAAT are known MUSMITAH مُصْمِتَة .

2. Besides the LETTERS of MU<u>Z</u>LIQAH the REST are the LETTERS of MU<u>S</u>MITAH.

B. THERE ARE SEVEN TYPES OF GHAIR MUTADHAADDAH:

1. QALQALAH   .قَلْقَلَه   2. <u>S</u>AFEER   .صَفِيْر

3. TAFASHSHEE   .تَفَشِّيْ   4. TAKREER   .تَكْرِيْر

5. LEEN   .لِيْن   6. IN<u>H</u>IRAAF   .اِنْحِرَاف

7. ISTI<u>T</u>ALAT   .اِسْتِطَالَتْ

1. **QALQALAH** قَلْقَلَه is that quality which when pronounced the VOICE of the letter (WHEN IT HAS A SUKOON) will be pronounced WITH AN ECHOING SOUND.

   e.g. The ق in خَلَقَ، خَلَقْنَا.

NOTE: There are five LETTERS of QALQALAH, which are قُطُبْ جَدٍّ.

2. **<u>S</u>AFEER** صَفِيْر is that quality which when pronounced the VOICE of the letter will be pronounced QUICKLY WITH A SOUND LIKE THAT OF A WHISTLE

   e.g. The س in مُسْلِمِيْنَ، اَسْلَمُوْا.

NOTE: There are three LETTERS of <u>S</u>AFEER, which are ز س ص.

3. **TAFASHSHEE** تَفَشِّيْ is that quality which when pronounced the VOICE of the letter will FLOW THROUGHOUT THE MOUTH.

   e.g. The ش in وَاَشْهَدَهُمْ قُرَيْشٍ.

NOTE: This quality if found ONLY IN THE LETTER

4. **TAKREER** تَكْرِيْر is that quality, which when pronounced there will be a shiver on the tongue.

e.g. The ر in اَلرَّحْمٰنُ، مَرْیَمَ.

IMPORTANT: Takreer is shown for this reason that a person should refrain from it.

NOTE: This quality is found only in the letter.

5. **LEEN** لِیْن is that quality, which when pronounced the VOICE of the letters if SO SOFT that if a person wants TO MAKE MADD ON THEM it will be POSSIBLE

e.g. The و in خَوْفٍ and the ی in وَالصَّیْفِ.

NOTE: 1. This quality is found ONLY in the LETTERS of LEEN.

2. و and ی will be the LETTERS of LEEN only when they have a sukoon and the letter before them has a zabar (fathah).

e.g. The و in اَوْ and the ی in اِبْنَیْ.

6. **INHIRAAF** اِنْحِرَاف is that quality, which when pronounced the SOUND of the letter RETURNS IN THE MAKHRAJ.

e.g. The makhraj of ر when pronounced, RETURNS TOWARDS the makhraj Of LAAM and VOICE-versa.

NOTE: This quality if found ONLY in the LETTERS ر and ل.

7. **ISTITALAT** اِسْتِطَالَت is that quality, which when pronounced the VOICE of the letter will REMAIN FROM THE BEGINNING of the MAKHRAJ TILL THE END

e.g. The ض in وَلَاالضَّآلِّیْنَ.

NOTE: This quality is found ONLY in the LETTER ض.

QUESTIONS

1. What is the definition of Sifaat?

2. How many types of Sifaat are there?

3. a. What does Ẕaatiyah mean?

   b. Name the two types of Ẕaatiyah

4. Define Mutadhaaddah.

5. Give only the ten names of Mutadhaaddah.

6. a. What is the definition of Hams?

   b. Name the ten letters of Hams

7. What does Rikhwat mean?

8. What is the difference between Isti'la and Iṭbaaq?

9. What does Ghair Mutadhaaddah mean?

10. Give only the seven names of Ghair Mutadhaaddah.

11. Define Qalqalah.

12. What are the letters of Inḥiraaf?

13. a. Istiṭalat is found in which letter?

    b. Define Istiṭalat?

AADAAB OF THE HOLY Quraan

It should be known that true benefit can only be derived from something when all it's aadaab and etiquettes are carried out in full. The same applies to the Quraan. Some of the etiquettes of the Quraan are as follows:

1. To have wudhu.

2. Face the Qiblah.

3. Sit in a clean place.

4. Sit in a respectable posture.

5. Recite with humility.

6. Correct the intention.

7. Keep the pleasure of Allah in mind.

8. Concentrate during recital.

9. Do not allow the mind to stray.

10. To apply it before recital.

11. To make miswaak before recital.

12. To wear good, clean clothes.

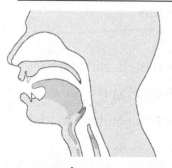

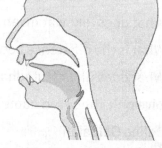

Makhraj of ز س The tip of the tongue when touching the edge of the edge of the thanaya Sufla including the Thanaya Ulya.

Sifaat Voice of letter should be soft and will flow in makhraj and will be pronounced sharply with a whistling sound.

Makhraj of د ت The tip of the tongue when touching the roots of the Thanaya Ulya Sifaat. Voice of letter should be hard and will end off in makhraj.

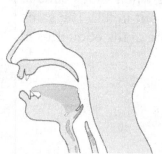

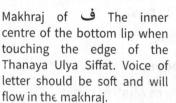

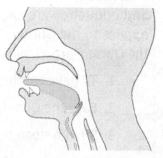

Makhraj of ف The inner centre of the bottom lip when touching the edge of the Thanaya Ulya Siffat. Voice of letter should be soft and will flow in the makhraj.

Makhraj of ذ ث The tip of the tongue when touching the edge of the Thanaya Ulya Sifaat. Voice of letter should be soft and will flow in makhraj.

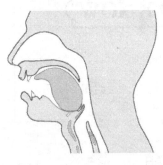 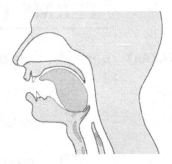

Makhraj of ض The back edge of the Tongue upturned touching the gums of the Molars and Premolars, Sifaat. Back of tongue.

should rise towards palate while the centre will meet and embrace it, and also sound of the letter will remain from beginning tili end of makhraj.

Makhraj of ص The tip of the tongue Touching the edge of the Thanaya Sufla including the Thanaya Ulya. Back of Tongue should rise Towards the paiare while the centre will meet and embrace it.

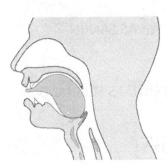 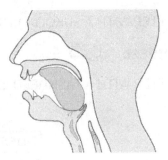

Makhraj of ظ The tip of the tongue when touching the edge of the Thanaya Ulya Sifaat. Back of tongue should rise towards the palate while the centre will meet and embrace it and voice will flow in makhraj.

Makhraj of ط The tip of the tongue when Touching the roots of the Thanaya Ulya Sifaat. Back of Tongue should rise towards the palate while the centre will meet and embrace it.

TERMS TO KNOW

HARAKAAT حَرَكَاتُ **are three:**

ZABAR	زَبَرْ	FATHAH	فَتْحَه	ـَ
ZER	زِير	KASRAH	كَسَرَة	ـِ
PESH	پِيْش	DHAMMAH	ضَمَّه	ـُ

A letter with a harkat is known as a MUTAHARRIK.

TANWEEN تَنْوِيْن **are also three.**

FATHATAIN	فَتْحَتَيْن	DO ZABAR	دُو	ـً
KASRATAIN	كَسَرَتَيْن	DO ZER	دُو	ـٍ
DHAMMATAIN	ضَمَّتَيْن	DO PESH	دُو	ـٌ

SUKOON سُكُوْن **JAZM** جَزْم ـْ

A LETTER WITH A SUKOON IS KNOWN AS SAAKIN

TASHDEED تَشْدِيْد ـّ

A LETTER WITH A TASHDEED IS KNOWN AS MUSHADDAD

QUESTIONS

1. Name the three Harkats.

2. How many tanween are there name them?

3. What is a Saakin and mushaddad?

(SIFAAT-E-'AARIDHAH)

1. The **LETTERS of MUSTA'LIYAH** مُسْتَعْلِيَهْ are seven:

خُصَّ ضَغْطٍ قِظْ

NOTE: These letters in every condition will be recited with a FULL MOUTH (MUFAKHKHAM).

EXAMPLES OF THE LETTERS OF MUSTA'LIYAH

1.	خَبِيْرٌ	خ
2.	صَلَحَ	ص
3.	ضَرَبَ	ض
4.	غَيْرِ	غ
5.	طَبَعَ	ط
6.	قَلِيْلُ ص	ق
7.	ظُفُرٍ ج	ظ

2. Besides the **LETTERS OF MUSTA'LIYAH**, the remaining are the **LETTERS OF MUSTAFILAH**.

NOTE: These letters in every condition will be recited with and EMPTY MOUTH, (MURAQQAQ).

EXAMPLES OF SOME OF THE LETTERS OF MUSTAFILAH:

1.	ثَوَابَ	ث
2.	جَمِيْلُ	ج
3.	دَرَجَةٌ	د
4.	مَازَاغَ	ز

5.	سَلَمًا	س
6.	شَكَرَ	ش
7.	لِفَتْهُ	ف

From the LETTERS OF MUSTAFILAH there are three LETTERS ا ل ر which are sometimes recited MUFAKHKHAM مُفَخَّم and sometimes recited MURAQQAQ مُرَقَّق.

QUESTIONS

1. How should the letters of Musta'liyah be read?

2. How will the letters of Mustafilah be read?

3. Which letters will sometimes be read Mufakhkham or sometimes muraqqaq?

THE RULES OF ALIF

1. If before AN ALIF there is a MUFAKHKHAM LETTER then that ALIF will also be recited with a FULL MOUTH

2. If before AN ALIF there is a MURAQQAQ LETTER then that ALIF will also be recited with an EMPTY MOUTH·

EXAMPLES OF THE SEVEN LETTERS OF MUSTA'LIYAH:

1.	خَالِدًا	خ
2.	صِلِحٌ	ص
3.	وَلَا الضَّآلِّينَ	ض
4.	غَافِرٍ	غ
5.	طٰه	ط
6.	قَاتِلُوا	ق
7.	ظَالِمَةٌ	ظ

EXAMPLES OF SOME OF THE LETTERS OF MUSTAFILAH

1.	ٱلۡبَاطِنُ	بِٱلۡبَاطِلِ	ب
2.	قَالَتَا	تَارِكُ	ت
3.	وَٱلضُّحَىٰ	حِفِظُوا	ح
4.	سَاقَيۡهَا	مُرۡسٰهَا	س
5.	وَمَشَارِبُ	شَاخِصَةٌ	ش
6.	دُعَآءِ ئِ	ٱلۡعٰلَمِينَ	ع
7.	تَكَادُ	كَانَ	ك

THE RULES OF BOTH THE LAAMS ل IN THE NAME OF ALLAH

1. If before the two ل in Allah there is a letter with a ZABAR (FAT<u>H</u>AH) or a PESH (DHAMMAH), then both the ل will be recited mufakhkham (fullmouth).

2. If before the two ل in ALLAH there is a ZER (K ASRAH) then both the ل will be recited MURAQQAQ (EMPTY MOUTH).

EXAMPLES OF THE NAME OF ALLAH الله BEFORE IT A LETTER WITH A:

A.	ZABAR-FAT<u>H</u>AH	عِنْدَاللهِ	سُبْحٰنَكَ اللّٰهُمَّ
B.	PESH-DHAMMAH	وَاتَّقُوا اللهَ	وَاِذْقَالُوا اللّٰهُمَّ
C.	ZER-KASRAH	بَلِ اللهُ	قُلِ اللّٰهُمَّ

QUESTIONS

1. When will the alif be read Mufakhkham?

2. Give some examples of the alif when it will be read mufakhkham?

3. When will the two ل in الله be read mufakhkham or muraqqaq?

4. How should these examples be read?

   1. وَاتَّقُوا اللهَ   2. عِنْدَاللهِ

   3. سُبْحٰنَكَ اللّٰهُمَّ   4. بَلِ اللهُ

THE RULES OF RAA ر

THE RAA ر MAS THREE CONDITIONS:

A. RAA MUTAHARRIK: The Raa ر will have any of the three HARKATS.

e.g.   رِجَالٌ   رُسُلٌ   رَبَّنَا

B. RAA SAAKIN, BEFORE IT A MUTAHARRIK: The RAA with a JAZM (SUKOON), the letter before it will have a HARKAT.

e.g.   مَرْيَمَ   اَلْفِرْدَوْسَ   مُرْسَلًا

C. RAA SAAKIN BEFORE IT A SAAKIN BEFORE THAT A MUTAHARRIK: The RAA with a JAZM, the letter before it will have a JAZM, and before that the letter will have a HARKAT.

e.g.   وَالْفَجْرِ   بِجِرٍ   خُسْرٍ

A. THE RULES OF RAA MUTAHARRIK.

1. If the RAA has a ZABAR or a PESH the RAA will be reacted WITH A FULL MOUTH.

2. If the RAA has a ZER, the RAA will be recited WITH AN EMPTY MOUTH.

EXAMPLES OF RAA ر ON IT A:

A. ZABAR-FATHAH   رَبُّكَ   رَسُوْلٌ

B. PESH-DHAMMAH   رُسُلًا   سُرُرُ

C. ZER-KASRAH   رِزْقًا   وَلَوْ كَرِهَ

B. THE RULES OF RAA SAAKIN ر BEFORE IT A MUTAHARRIK.

1. If the MUTAHARRIK before the RAA SAKIN has a FATHAH or a DHAMMAH the RAA will be recited WITH A FULL MOUTH.

2. If the MUTA_HARRIK before the RAA SAAKIN has a KASRAH THE RAA will be recited WITH AN EMPTY MOUTH.

EXAMPLES OF A RAA SAAKIN, BEFORE IT A LETTER WITH A:

A. ZABAR-FAT_HAH   اَرۡسَلَ   اَقۡرَرۡنَا

B. PESH-DHAMMAH   وَاذۡكُرۡ   تُرۡجَعُونَ

C. ZER-KASRAH   يَسۡتَغۡفِرۡلَكُمۡ   وَكَفِّرۡعَنَّا

NOTE: There are THREE CONDITION for this RAA to be recited MURAQQAQ:

2.1 Before the RAA SAAKIN the KASRAH should be A_SLI (ORIGINAL) AND NOT 'AARDHI (TEMPORARY). Therefore if the KASRAH is 'AARDHI (TEMPORARY) the RAA will be recited WITH A FULL MOUTH.

EXAMPLES OF KASRAH-E-A_SLI: بِشِرۡكِكُمۡ

EXAMPLES OF KASRAH-E-'AARDHI: اِرۡجِعُوۡ   اِرۡجِعِيۤ

2.2 Before the RAA SAAKIN the KASRAH will be in the same word and NOT in the PRECEDING word. Therefore if the KASRAH is in the PRECEDING word then the RAA WILL NOT be recited MURAQQAQ but will be recited MUFAKHKHAM.

EXAMPLES OF KASRAH BEING IN THE SAME WORD.

اَنۡذِرۡهُمۡ   يَغۡفِرۡلَكُمۡ

EXAMPLES OF KASRAH BEING IN THE PRECEDING WORD.

رَبِّ ارۡجِعُوۡنِ   اَمِ ارۡتَابُوۡا

2.3 After the RAA SAAKIN none of the LETTERS OF MUSTA'LIYAH must be found in the same word. If there is a LETTER OF MUSTA'LIYAH in the same word the RAA WILL NOT be recited MURAQQAQ but it will be recited MUFAKHKHAM.

EXAMPLES OF THE LETTERS OF MUSTA'LIYAH BEING IN THE SAME WORD:

فِرْقَةٍ   قِرْطَاسٍ   اِرْصَادًا   مِرْصَادًا

NOTE: 1. These are the only examples in the Quraan-e-kareem.

2. In كُلُّ فِرْقٍ the raa can be recited both muraqqaq and mufakhkham. Those Qaris who took into consideration both the kasrah on either side of the Raa recited it Muraqqaq. And those Qaris who took into consideration that the letter of Isti'la appears after the Raa Saakin, recited it Mufakhkham.

C. THE RULES OF RAA SAAKIN, BEFORE IT A SAAKIN BEFORE THAT A MUTA<u>H</u>ARRIK

1. If the MUTA<u>H</u>ARRIK has a FAT<u>H</u>AH or a DHAMMAH then the RAA Will be recited MUFAKHKHAM

2. If the MUTA<u>H</u>ARRIK has a KASRAH then the RAA will be recited MURAQQAQ. THUS THE RULE IS that if before the raa saakin besides the yaa saakin any other letter with a saakin appears and before it the muta<u>h</u>arrik has a fat ha or a dhammah then the raa will be recited mufakhkham and if the muta<u>h</u>arrik has a kasrah then the raa will be recited muraqqaq

e.g.   FAT<u>H</u>AH   وَالْفَجْرِ   مَعَ الْأَبْرَارِ   وَالْعَصْرِ

DHAMMAH   لَفِيْ خُسْرٍ   مِنْ نُّوْرٍ   بِكُمُ الْعُسْرَ

KASRAH   لِنَبِيْ حِجْرٍ   وَلَابِكْرُ   نَسُوا الذِّكْرَ

3. If before the RAA SAAKIN there is a YAA SAAKIN then that RAA UNDER EVERY CONDITION (WHETHER THE MUTA<u>H</u>ARRIK HAS A FAT HA DHAMMAH OR A KASRAH) will be recited MURAQQAQ ONLY.

e.g. The لَاضَيْرَ فِيْهَاخَيْرُ وَالطَّيْرَ
اِلَّا اَنْ نِّيْرُ وَنِعْمَ النَّصِيْرُ

4. After RAA there is only one (1) place in the QURAAN مَّجْرِىهَا in surah hood in which IMAM HAFS (RAHMATULLAHI 'ALAIH) makes IMAALAH اِمَالَهُ Because of IMAALAH this RAA will be recited Muraqqaq.

THE RULES OF RAA MUSHADDAD رّ

The rules of RAA MUSHADDAD is the SAME as that of RAA MUTAHARRIK. If the RAA MUSHADDAD has FATHAH or a DHAMMAH the RAA will be recited MUFAKHKHAM And if the RAA MUSHADDAD has a KASRAH the RAA will be recited MURAQQAQ.

e.g. مِنْ شَرِّ حَرَّمَ اللّٰهُ مُسْتَقَرُّ

QUESTIONS

1. Name the three conditions of Raa.

2. a. What are the rules of Raa Mutaharrik?

   b. Give examples.

3. a. Explain the rules of Raa Saakin before it a Mutaharrik.

   b. Give examples.

4. a. Mention the three conditions for the raa Saakin to be read Muraqqaq?

   b. And also write the examples in each condition?

5. Describe the rule of Raa Saakin before it a saakin and before that a Mutaharrik?

6. How will the raa in the word مَّجْرِىهَا be read?

THE RULES OF MEEM MUSHADDAD مّ
AND NOON MUSHADDAD نّ

If there is a TASHDEED on a MEEM مّ or a NOON نّ then the MEEM and NOON will be recited with GHUNNAH.

e.g. مِمَّا مِمَّ عَمَّيكَ ثُمَّ بِهِنَّ كُلُّهُنَّ عَلَيْهِنَّ اِنَّ الظَّنَّ اِنَّ

NOTE: The duration of GHUNNAH is ONE ALIF.

THE RULES OF MEEM SAAKIN مْ

MEEM SAAKIN HAS THREE RULES:

1. IDGHAAM اِدْغَامُ

2. IKHFAA اِخْفَاءُ

3. IZH-HAAR اِظْهَارُ

1. IDGHAAM اِدْغَامُ

If after MEEM SAAKIN مْ there appears a MEEM م IDGHAAM with GHUNNAH will take place.

2. IKHFAA اِخْفَاءُ

If after MEEM SAAKIN مْ there appears the letter BAA بIKHFAA will take place.

e.g. وَمَنْ يَّعْتَصِمْ بِاللّٰهِ   رُسُلُهُمْ بِالْبَيِّنٰتِ   عَلَيْهِمْ بَرَكٰتٍ

NOTE: This IKHFAA is known as IKHFAA-E-SHAFAWI.

3. IZH-HAAR اِظْهَارُ

If after MEEM SAAKIN مْ besides the letters MEEM AND BAA بany other letter appears. IZH-HAAR will take place.

e.g. عَلَيْهِمْ وَلَا الضَّآلِّيْنَ هُمْ يُوْقِنُوْنَ اٰمْهِلْهُمْ رُوَيْدًا كَيْدَهُمْ فِيْ

NOTE: This IZH-HAAR is known as IZH-HAAR-E-SHAFAWI.

QUESTIONS

1. What is the duration of Ghunnah?

2. How many rules has Meem Saakin got?

3. Define Idghaam and Ikhfaa.

4. How will these words be read.

2. رُسُلُهُمْ بِالْبَيِّنٰتِ   1. اٰمْهِلْهُمْ رُوَيْدًا

4. كَيْدَهُمْ فِيْ   3. لَهُمْ مُّوْسٰى

NOON SAAKIN AND TANWEEN HAS FOUR RULES:

1. IZH-HAAR اِظْهَار
2. IDGHAAM اِدْغَام
3. QALB قَلْب
4. IKHFAA اِخْفَاء

1. IZH-HAAR اِظْهَار

NOTE: The common meaning of IZH-HAAR is to pronounce the letters from their MAKHRAJ CLEARLY AND DISTINCTLY without any changes.

If after NOON SAAKIN نْ OR TANWEEN ـًـٍـٌ any of LETTERS OF HUROOF-E-HALQI خ غ ع ح ه ء appear there will be IZH-HAAR اِظْهَار

e.g.

	ـُ	ـِ	ـَ	ل	ن
ء	وَمِنْ اَهْلِ	وَيَنْئَوْنَ	اِذَا اَبَدًا	بِعَذَابٍ اَلِيمٍ	عَذَابٌ اَلِيمٌ
ه	وَمِمَّنْ هَدَيْنَا	مِنْهُمْ	فَرِيقًا هَدَى	قَوْمٍ هَادٍ	اِنِ امْرُؤٌا هَلَكَ
ع	مِنْ عِبَادِنَا	اَنْعَمْتَ	قُرْءٰنًا عَرَبِيًّا	بِكَافٍ عَبْدَهُ	عَرْشٌ عَظِيمٌ
ح	مِنْ حَيْثُ	وَتَنْحِتُوْنَ	عَلِيمًا حَكِيمًا	بِاَلْسِنَةٍ حِدَادٍ	اَرْبَعَةٌ حُرُمٌ
غ	مِنْ غَيْرِ	فَسَيُنْغِضُوْنَ	عَفُوًّا غَفُوْرًا	سَفِينَةٍ غَصْبًا	لَعَفُوٌّ غَفُوْرٌ
خ	مِنْ خَشْيَةٍ	وَالْمُنْخَنِقَةُ	عَلِيمًا خَبِيْرًا	كَاذِبَةٍ خَاطِئَةٍ	وَرَحْمَةٌ خَيْرٌ

This IZH-HA AR is known as IZH-HAAR-E-HALQI

2. IDGHAAM اِدْغَام

NOTE: The common meaning of IDGHAAM is to enter one thing into another

If after NOON SAAKIN نْ OR TANWEEN ـًـٍـٌ any of the SIX

LETTERS OF YARMALOON يَرْمَلُوْنَ appears then there will be IDGHAAM. In LAAM AND RAA the IDGHAAM will be COMPLETE, which is known as IDGHAAM-E-TAAM

e.g.

ل	مِنْ لَّدُنْ	خَيْرًا لَّهُمْ	لَا يٰتٍ لِّقَوْمٍ	وَيْلٌ لِّكُلِّ

ر	مِنْ رَّحْمَتِهِ	تَوَّابًا رَّحِيْمًا	عِيْشَةٍ رَّاضِيَةٍ	غَفُوْرٌ رَّحِيْمٌ

In the remaining four letters و م ن ى

يَنْمُوْ the IDGHAAM will be INCOMPLETE, which is known as IDGHAAM-E-NAAQIS اِدْغَامِ نَاقِص

NOTE: IDGHAAM IN THIS INSTANCE WILL BE WITH GHUNNAH

e.g.

ن ى	وَمَنْ يَّعْمَلْ	مُنَادِيًا يُّنَادِى	لِقَوْمٍ يَّعْلَمُوْنَ	رِجَالٌ يُّحِبُّوْنَ

ن	مِنْ نُّصِرِيْنَ	رَسُوْلًا نَّبِيًّا	يَوْمَئِذٍ نَّاعِمَةٌ	طَلْعٌ نَّضِيْدٌ

م	مِنْ مَّقَامِكَ	اَيَّامًا مَّعْدُوْدٰتٍ	سُرُرٍ مَّوْضُوْنَةٍ	قُرْاٰنٌ مَّجِيْدٌ

و	مِنْ وَّرَقَةٍ	جَنَّةً وَّحَرِيْرًا	جَنّٰتٍ وَّعُيُوْنٍ	نَفْخَةٌ وَّاحِدَةٌ

There will be no IDGHAAM in the following words:

بُنْيَانٌ   صِنْوَانٌ   قِنْوَانٌ   اَلدُّنْيَا

Since the NOON SAAKIN نْ and ى or و are in the me word.

3. QALB قَلْب

NOTE: The literal meaning of QALB is to change one thing into another.

If after NOON SAAKIN نْ OR TANWEEN ًٌٍ the letter ب appears, then that NOON SAAKIN OR TANWEEN will change into a MEEM SAAKIN and will be recited WITH GHUNNAH,

e.g. ﹹ   ﹻ   ﹷ   ن

4. IKHFAA اِخْفَاء

NOTE: The literal meaning of IKHFA is to conceal if after NOON SAAKIN نْ OR TANWEEN ﹹ besides the SIX LETTERS OF HUROOF-E-HALQI ء ھ ع ح غ خ the SIX LETTERS OF YARMALOON يَرْمَلُوْنَ and THE LETTER ب if any other letter appears then the NOON SAAKIN OR TANWEEN will be recited with IKHFAA.

e.g.

حُرُوْفِ اِخْفَاء	نْ	نْ	ﹷ	ﹻ	ﹹ
ت	اَنْ تَتَّقُوْا	وَاَنْتُمْ	نَارًا تَلَظّٰى	خَيْرٌ تَجِدُوْهُ	قَوْمٌ تَجْهَلُوْنَ
ث	مَنْ ثَقُلَتْ	بِالْاُنْثٰى	مَاءً ثَجَّاجًا	يَوْمَئِذٍ ثَمَانِيَةٌ	شِهَابٌ ثَاقِبٌ
ج	مِنْ جِنَّةٍ	فَاَنْجَيْنٰهُ	ظَلُوْمًا جَهُوْلًا	اُمَّةٌ جَعَلْنَا	عَيْنٌ جَارِيَةٌ
د	مِنْ دُوْنِ	عِنْدَ اللّٰهِ	دَكًّا دَكًّا	وَلِكُلٍّ دَرَجٰتٌ	دُرٌّ دَعَانَا
ذ	مِمَّنْ ذَا الَّذِيْ	اَلْمُنْذِرِيْنَ	نَارًا ذَاتَ	سِلْسِلَةٍ ذَرْعُهَا	عَزِيْزٌ ذُوانْتِقَامٍ
ز	مَنْ زَكّٰهَا	اُنْزِلَ	وَطَرًا زَوَّجْنٰكَهَا	بَعْضٍ زُخْرُفٍ	حَمِيْدٌ زَعَمَ
س	عَنْ سَبِيْلِه	يٰۤاَيُّهَا الْاِنْسَانُ	قَوْلًا سَدِيْدًا	لَيَالٍ سَوِيًّا	كَلِمَةٌ سَبَقَتْ
ش	فَمَنْ شَاءَ	وَتَنْشَقُّ	سَبْعًا شِدَادًا	شَيْءٍ شَهِيْدٌ	غَفُوْرٌ شَكُوْرٌ
ص	وَلَمَنْ صَبَرَ	فَاَنْصُرْنَا	عَنْاَبًا صَعَدًا	بِرِيْحٍ صَرْصَرٍ	رِجَالٌ صَدَقُوْا
ض	عَنْ ضَيْفٍ	مَنْضُوْدٍ	قَوْمًا ضَالِّيْنَ	لِكُلٍّ ضِعْفٌ	ذُرِّيَّةٌ ضُعَفَاءُ
ط	مَنْ طَفٰى	اِنْطَلِقُوْ	كَلِمَةً طَيِّبَةً	سَمٰوٰتٍ طِبَاقًا	بَلْدَةٌ طَيِّبَةٌ
ظ	اِنْ ظَنَّا	تَنْظُرُوْنَ	ظِلًّا ظَلِيْلًا	نَفْسٍ ظَلَمَتْ	سَحَابٌ ظُلُمٰتٌ
ف	مِنْ فَضْلٍ	فِیْۤ اَنْفُسِكُمْ	قَوْمًا فٰسِقِيْنَ	بِهَدِيَّةٍ فَنٰظِرَةٌ	مُحْسِنٌ فَلَهُ
ق	مِنْ قَبْلِكَ	لَمُنْقَلِبُوْنَ	ثَمَنًا قَلِيْلًا	عَالِيَةٍ قُطُوْفُهَا	فَيَؤُسٌ قَنُوْطٌ
ك	وَلٰكِنْ كَانُوْا	وَاِنْ مِنْكُمْ	كِرَامًا كَاتِبِيْنَ	اَكْوَابٍ كَانَتْ	عَدَاوَةٌ كَاَنَّهُ

QUESTIONS

1. Name the four rules of Noon Saakin and Tanween?
2. Give the common and technical meaning of Idghaam?
3. What does Idghaame Naqi<u>s</u> and Idghaame Taam mean?
4. Give some examples of words in which Idghaam will be Naqi<u>s</u>?
5. Why will there be no Idghaam in the following words?

   1. قِنۡوَانٌ   2. اَلدُّنۡيَا

   3. صِنۡوَانٌ   4. بُنۡيَانٌ

6. Describe the rule of Qalb with examples?
7. When will Ikhfa take place?

AADAAB OF THE HOLY QURAAN

It should be known that true benefit can only be derived from something when all it's aadaab and etiquettes are carried out in full. The same applies to the Quraan. Some of the etiquettes of the Quraan are as follows:

1. Not to talk to anyone during recital.
2. If speech is necessary, to recite a'UZU when recommencing tilawat.
3. Quraan can either be recited loudly or softly, according to the circumstances.
4. Quraan could either be recited looking inside or by heart.
5. Quraan should be recited in a beautiful, melodious voice.
6. Recite the Quraan in the tone of the Arabs.

N.B. However the Laws of Tajweed must be observed under all circumstances.

THE RULES OF MADD

The common meaning of MADD is to extend a thing from it's original position.

The technical meaning of MADD is to prolong the letters of MADD OR LEEN.

There are TWO types of MADD.

A.   MADD-E-ASLI   مَدِّ اَصْلِیْ

B.   MADD-E-FAR'I   مَدِّ فَرْعِیْ

A.   MADD-E-ASLI   مَدِّ اَصْلِیْ

That MADD which after the LETTERS OF MADD there is no HAMZAH or SUKOON.

NOTE: 1.   The LETTERS OF MADD-E-ASLI مَدِّ اَصْلِیْ are THREE:

a.   An ALIF ا before it a letter with a FATHAH.

b.   A WAOW و before it a letter with a DHAMMAH.

c.   A YAA ى before it a letter with a KASRAH.

e.g.   اُوْذِيْنَا   وَاُوْتِيْنَا   نُوْحِيْهَا

2.   The duration of MADD-E-ASLI is ONE ALIF is NOT permissible to prolong the MADD-E-ASLI MORE than ONE ALIF nor is it correct to make this MADD LESS than ONE ALIF. To do so is HARAAM (because by prolonging more than an ALIF is adding a letter to the QURAAN and by making it less than an ALIF is reducing a letter from the QURAAN)

B.   MADD-E-FAR'I   مَدِّ فَرْعِیْ

That MADD which, after the LETTERS OF MADD, there is a HAMZAH ء OR SUKOON .

e.g.   مَآوٰى   بِضَآرِّيْنَ   هٰؤُلَاءِ   وَالْمَلٰئِكَةِ   آلْئٰنَ

There are FOUR types of MADD-E-FAR'I

a. MADD-E-MUTTAS̱IL مَدٍّ مُتَّصِلْ

b. MADD-E-MUNFAS̱IL مَدٍّ مُنْفَصِلْ

c. MADD-E-'AARIDH WAQFI مَدٍّ عَارِضْ وَقْفِیْ

d. MADD-E-LAAZIM مَدٍّ لَازِمْ

a. MADD-E-MUTTAS̱IL مَدٍّ مُتَّصِلْ

That MADD which after the LETTERS OF MADD the HAMZAH appears in the SAME WORD.

e.g.

يَشَآء	وَالْقَآئِلِیْنَ	جَآءَ	ا
لَتَنُوْٓءُ	مِنْ سُوْٓءٍ	السُّوْٓءَ	و
یُضِیْٓءُ	وَجَآئَ ءَ		ی

NOTE: The duration of MADD-E-MUTTAS̱IL is 2-2½ or 4 ALIFS - which is known as TAWASSUṮ تَوَسُّطْ.

b. MADD-E-MUNFAS̱IL مَدٍّ مُنْفَصِلْ

That MADD which, after the LETTERS OF MADD the HAMZAH appears at the BEGINNING OF THE SECOND WORD.

e.g.

كَمَآ أُمِرْتَ	فَأَوْحٰیٓ اِلٰی	عَلٰیٓ اٰثَارِهِمَا	ا
قَالُوْٓا اُوْذِیْنَا	تُوْبُوْٓا اِلَیْهِ	وَاشْهَدُوْٓا اَنِّیْ	و
بِعَهْدِیْٓ اُوْفِ	وَیَهْدِیٓ اِلَیْهِ	وَتَرْحَمْنِیٓ اَکُنْ	ی

NOTE: The duration of MADD-E-MUNFA'IL is according to IMA AM SHATBI اِمَامْ شَاطِبِیْ 2-2½ OR 4 ALIF which is known as TAWASSUṮ

c. MADD-E-'AARIDH WAQFI مَدِّ عَارِضْ وَقْفِي

That MADD which after the LETTERS OF MADD, the HARKAT of the LAST LETTER of the word will be CHANGED into a SUKOON which is TEMPORARY due to stopping.

e.g.

ا	خَلَقَ الْإِنْسَانَ	فِي الْمِيْزَانِ	لَهُمُ الْأَبْوَابَ
و	فَاِلَيْهِ تُجْزَرُوْنَ	وَاِيَّاىَ فَارْهَبُوْنِ	كُنْ فَيَكُوْنُ
ى	لِلْعٰلَمِيْنَ	صِرَاطٍ مُّسْتَقِيْمٍ	لَرَءُوْفٌ رَّحِيْمٌ

NOTE:
1. The duration of MADD-E-'AARIDH WAQFI is TOOL طُوْلْ TAWASSUT تَوَسُّطْ and QASR قَصْر.

2. TOOL will get preference, then TAWASSUT thereafter QASR.

3. The duration of TOOL is 3 or 5 ALIFS TAWASSUT is 2 or 3 ALIFS, QASR is 1 ALIF.

NOTE:
1. In MADD-E-LEEN 'AARIDH, there will be QASR THEN TAWASSUT THEN TOOL.

2. The duration in MADD-E-LEEN 'AARIDH of QASR is 1 HARKAT (HALF AN ALIF). TAWASSUT is 1 OR 1 ½ ALIFS and TOOL is 2-2 ½ OR 3 ALIFS.

Examples of MADD-E-LEEN 'AARIDH:

| و | عَلَيْكُمُ الْيَوْمَ | مِنْ خَوْفٍ | وَلَا نَوْمٌ |
| ى | اُنْظُرْ اِلَيْكَ | وَالصَّيْفِ | ذٰلِكَ خَيْرٌ |

d. MADD-E-LAAZIM مَدِّ لَازِمْ

That MADD which, after the LETTERS OF MADD, the SUKOON is ORIGINAL أَصْلِي.

49

NOTE: SUKOON-E-A<u>S</u>LI is that SUKOON which remains in the word whether stopping or not.

There are FOUR types of MADD-E-LAAZIM مَدِّلَازِمِ

    a.   KILMI MUTHAQQAL كِلْمِیْ مُثَقَّلْ

    b.   KILMI MUKHAFFAF كِلْمِیْ مُخَفَّفْ

    c.   <u>H</u>ARFI MUTHAQQAL حَرْفِیْ مُثَقَّلْ

    d.   <u>H</u>ARFI MUKHAFFAF حَرْفِیْ مُخَفَّفْ

a. KILMI MUTHAQQAL كِلْمِیْ مُثَقَّلْ

That MADD which after the LETTERS OF MADD there is a TASHDEED, and BOTH, the LETTER OF MADD AND TASHDEED are in ONE WORD.

e.g.   اَتُحَآجُّوْنِّی   فَسَئَلِ الْعَآدِّیْنَ   ضَآلِّیْنَ

لَرَآدُّكَ   دَآبَّةٍ   یُحَآدُّوْنَ اللهَ   وَالصَّٓقَّتِ

اَلْحَآقَّةُ   مَا الْحَآقَّةُ   وَخَلَقَ الْجَآنَّ   بِضَآرِّیْنَ

b. KILMI MUKHAFFAF كِلْمِیْ مُخَفَّفْ

That MADD which, after the LETTERS OF MADD there is a SUKOON and BOTH, the LETTER OF MADD SUKOON are in ONE WORD.

e.g.   آلْـٰٔنَ

NOTE: This is the ONLY example in the QURAAN of KILMI MUKHAFFAF.

c. <u>H</u>ARFI MUTHAQQAL حَرْفِیْ مُثَقَّلْ

That MADD which, after the LETTERS OF MADD there is a TASHDEED, and BOTH, the LETTER OF MADD and THE LETTERS OF MUQA<u>TT</u>A'AAT مُقَطَّعَاتْ.

e.g.   الٓمّٓ   الٓمّٓرٰ   طٰسٓمّٓ

d. HARFI MUKHAFFAF حَرْفِي مُخَفَّفْ

That MADD which, after the LETTERS OF MADD there is a SUKOON, and BOTH, the LETTERS OF MADD and the LETTERS OF MUQATTA'AAT مُقَطَّعَاتْ.

e.g.   الٓرٰ   يٰسٓ   حٰمٓ   قٓ   طٰسٓ

نٓ وَالْقَلَمِ   كٓهٰيٰعٓصٓ   حٰمٓ عٓسٓقٓ   صٓ وَالْقُرْاٰنِ

NOTE: 1. In all FOUR type of MADD-E-LAAZIM there will ONLY be TOOL طُوْل.

2. The duration of TOOL طُوْل is 3 or 5 ALIFS.

LEEN-E-LAAZIM لِيْنِ لَازِمْ

If after the LETTERS OF LEEN a SUKOON-E-ASLI سُكُوْنِ اَصْلِي appears, then that LETTERS OF LEEN will be known as LEEN-E-LAAZIM.

EXAMPLE: The ع in حٰمٓ عٓسٓقٓ and كٓهٰيٰعٓصٓ In LEEN-E-LAAZIM, there will be TOOL طُوْل.

TAWASSUT تَوَسُّطْ and QASR قَصْر TOOL will get preference, then TAWASSUT and QASR is very weak.

QUESTIONS

1. What is the common and technical meaning of Madd?

2. How many types of Madd are there?

3. When will the letters ا،و،ی be letters of Madd?

4. What is the duration of Madd-e-Asli?

5. What is Madd-e-Far'i?

6. Name the four types of Madd-e-Far'i?

7. a. Define Madd-e-Muttasil and Madd-e-Munfasil?

b. Give examples of both Madds?

c. What are the durations of these Madds?

8. a. What is Madd-e-'Aaridh waqfi?

    b. Give some examples of Madd-e-'Aaridh Waqfi?

    c. What is the duration of this Madd?

9. Name the four types of Madd-e-Laazim?

10. Define Kilmi Muthaqqal and Harfi Mukhaffaf?

11. Give some examples of Kilmi Mukhaffaf and Harfi Muthaqqal?

12. What is the duration in all four types of Madd-e-Laazim?

13. What is Leen-e-Laazim?

THE RULES OF WAQF (STOPPING)

The common meaning of waqf is to stop.

The technical meaning is to stop on such a complete word which is separate from the word after it pausing so long as is sufficient to take in a new breath, and to have the intention of reading forward.

There are three types of waqf.

1. Waqf in which the condition of the LAST LETTER IS considered.

2. Waqf in which the PLACE of stopping is considered.

3. Waqf in which the CONDITION of the QARI is considered.

There are three types of كَيْفِيَتِ وَقْف

1. Waqf bil Iskaan وَقْف بِالْإِسْكَان

2. Waqf bil Ishmaam وَقْف بِالْإِشْمَام

3. Waqf bil Raum وَقْف بِالرَّوْم

1. **Waqf bil Iskaan** is to make waqf on the last letter of the word making it a saakin in such a way that the harkat is not read nor is there an indication by the lips towards the harkat. This waqf is possible on all three harkat's (zabar, zer, pesh). Whether the harkat is Asli (original) or 'Aardhi (temporary), whether the word has a tanween or not and this waqf is possible on the round Taa.

e.g. of Haarkat-e-Asli

حَكِيْمٌ عَلِيْمٌ	حَكِيْمٌ عَلِيْمٌ	هُمُ الصَّادِقُوْنَ	هُمُ الصَّادِقُوْنَ
خُلُقٍ عَظِيْمٍ	خُلُقٍ عَظِيْمٍ	هٰذَا يَوْمُ الدِّيْنِ	هٰذَا يَوْمُ الدِّيْنِ
نَخْلٍ خَاوِيَةٌ	نَخْلٍ خَاوِيَةٍ	وَهُوَالْخَلَّقُ الْعَلِيْمُ	وَهُوَالْخَلَّقُ الْعَلِيْمُ
أُذُنٌ وَّاعِيَةٌ	أُذُنٌ وَّاعِيَةٌ	أَصْحٰبُ الْمَيْمَنَةِ	أَصْحٰبُ الْمَيْمَنَةِ

e.g. of <u>H</u>arkat-e-'Aardhi

مِنْ	مِنَ الثَّمَرَاتِ
عَلَيْكُمْ	عَلَيْكُمُ الصِّيَامُ
وَلَقَدْ	وَلَقَدِ اسْتُهْزِئَ

2. **Waqf bil Ishmaam** is to make waqf on the last letter of the word (in such a way as to) indicate by the lips to the <u>h</u>arkat that is on it. This waqf is possible on a Dhammah-e-A<u>s</u>li and not on a 'Aardhi Dhammah. It is possible on a word whether it has a tanween or not. This waqf is not possible on a round Taa.

e.g.

of Dhammah-e-A<u>s</u>li	وَهُوَ الْحَكِيْمُ الْخَبِيْرُ
of Dhammah-e-'Aardhi	عَلَيْكُمُ الْقِتَالُ
of Tanween	وَاِنَّمَا اَنَا نَذِيْرٌ مُّبِيْنٌ
of a Round Taa	اِذَا وَقَعَتِ الْوَاقِعَةُ

3. **Waqf bil Raum** is to make waqf on the last letter of the word reading the <u>h</u>arkat so softly that only those who are near are able to listen to it. This waqf is possible on a Dhammah and Kasrah, and is possible on a <u>h</u>arkat-e-A<u>s</u>li and not a <u>h</u>arkat-e-'Aardhi

e.g.

of <u>H</u>arkat-e-Asli	وَلَاتَ حِيْنَ مَنَاصٍ ۝ اَلرَّحْمٰنُ
of <u>H</u>arkat-e-'Aardhi	اَنَّهُمْ هُمُ الْفَائِزُوْنَ ۝ عَلَيْهِمُ الذِّلَّةُ
	اَنْ اَنْذِرِ النَّاسَ ۝ مَنِ اسْتَرَقَ

In the same way this waqf is not possible on a round Taa. ة

e.g. فَأُهْلِكُوا بِالطَّاغِيَةِ   مَا الْحَاقَّةُ

This waqf is possible on a word whether it has a tanween or not

e.g. إِنَّهُ لَمَجْنُونٌ   بِمَاءٍ مَّعِينٍ

There are four types of   مَحَلِّ وَقْف

    1. Waqf-e-TAAM   وَقْفِ تَامٌ

    2. Waqf-e-Kafi   وَقْفِ كَافِئ

    3. Waqf-e-<u>H</u>asan   وَقْفِ حَسَنٌ

    4. Waqf-e-Qabee<u>h</u>   وَقْفِ قَبِيحٌ

1. **Waqf-e-Taam** is to make waqf on such a place where the sentence is complete and there is on connection in the meaning of the word of this sentence and the one's preceding or proceeding it.

   e.g. وَأُولَٰئِكَ هُمُ الْمُفْلِحُونَ۞   إِيَّاكَ نَعْبُدُ وَإِيَّاكَ نَسْتَعِينُ۞

2. **Waqf-e-Kafi** is to make waqf on such a place where the sentence is complete, but there is a connection of only the meaning and not the word of the sentence preceding or proceeding it.

   e.g. رَزَقْنَٰهُمْ يُنفِقُونَ۞   هُدًى لِّلْمُتَّقِينَ۞

     وَبِالْآخِرَةِ هُمْ يُوقِنُونَ۞

3. **Waqf-e-<u>H</u>asan** is to make waqf in such a place where the sentence is complete, but there is a connection in both the meaning and word of this sentence and the one's preceding or proceeding it.

   e.g. To stop on:

ذٰلِكَ الۡكِتٰبُ   وَاعۡبُدُوا اللّٰهَ وَلَا تُشۡرِكُوۡا

4. **Waqf-e-Qabee<u>h</u>** is to make waqf on such a place where the sentence is incomplete and there is every type of connection with that which is preceding or following it and also the meaning is distorted.

e.g. To stop on:

يٰٓاَيُّهَا الَّذِيۡنَ اٰمَنُوۡا لَا تَقۡرَبُوا الصَّلٰوةَ   اِنَّ اللّٰهَ لَا يَسۡتَحۡيٖ

In Waqf-e-Taam and Kafi the reading will be initiated after stopping on the sentence, it will not be necessary to repeat.

If Waqf-e-<u>H</u>asan is made on a ayat than the reading will be initiated after the ayat otherwise it will be necessary to repeat.

In Waqf-e-Qabee<u>h</u> it will always be necessary to repeat.

There are four types of وَقۡفٌ بِاعۡتِبَارِ اَحۡوَالِ قَارِئٍ

1. Waqf-e-Ikhtiyari   وَقۡفٍ اِخۡتِيَارِئٍ

2. Waqf-e-Ikhtibari   وَقۡفٍ اِخۡتِبَارِئٍ

3. Waqf-e-Idhtirari   وَقۡفٍ اِضۡطِرَارِئٍ

4. Waqf-e-Intizhari   وَقۡفٍ اِنۡتِظَارِئٍ

1. **Waqf-e-Ikhtiyari** is a voluntary stop which is generally made to take in a new breath.

2. **Waqf-e-Ikhtibari** is an informative stop which is made with the intention of explaining how a stop is made on the last letter of a word.

3. **Waqf-e-Idh<u>t</u>irari** is an involuntary stop which is caused by an unplanned break in the breath, e.g. by a cough, shortness or breath or forgetting etc.

4. **Waqf-e-Intizhari** is to stop on a particular place repeatedly to complete the various Qiraat.

SAKTAH

Saktah is to keep the breath intact and to halt the voice temporally. The rules that apply to waqf (stooping) will be applied to Saktah as well.

There are four places in the Quraan where Saktah is Wajib.

1. In Surah Kahaf on   عِوَجًا ۜ قَيِّمًا

2. In Surah Yaseen on   مِنۡ مَّرۡقَدِنَا ۜ هٰذَا

3. In Surah Qiyamah on   وَقِيۡلَ مَنۡ ۜ رَاقٍ

4. In Surah Motaf-fefeen on   كَلَّا بَلۡ ۜ رَانَ

(MISCELLANEA)

1. There are some words in the Quraan in which the alif is written, but read only when stopping on them.

    e.g.   أَنَا۠ أَكْثَرُ   لَٰكِنَّا۠ هُوَ اللهُ

    a. When stopping on the word سَلْسِلَا۠ it is permissible both to read the alif and also to omit it.

    b. The word قَوَارِيرَا۠ appears twice in Surah Dahr.

The rule here is that if stooping on the first one then the alif will read, but in the second the alif will not be read at all, whether stopping or not.

2. There is one place in the Quraan in which Imalah is made i.e. مَجْرٖىٰهَا in Surah Hood.

3. In Surah Hameem Sajdah there is one place in which it is necessary to make Tasheel in the second Hamzah i.e. ءَاَعْجَمِيٌّ .

Tasheel means to read the Hamzah with a soft tone.

4. In these four words Idghaam will be Naqis

(incomplete)   مَا فَرَّطْتُّمْ   لَئِنۢ بَسَطتَّ

                مَا فَرَّطتُّ   فَقَالَ اَحَطتُّ

That means that the makhraj of ط will be incorporated into the ت but not the sifaat of Isti'la and Itbaaq, hence the ط will be read with **Tafkheem**, but without **Qalqalah**.

5. In Surah Yusuf the word اَلْكِتَابُ has to be read with Ishmaam or Raum. When making Ishmaam, Idghaam has to be made, and when making Raum Izh-haar has to be made.

Ishmaam means to indicate by the lips towards the Dhammah.

Raum means to read one third of a <u>h</u>arkat.

6. There are four words in the Quraan which are written with a ص and on this there is a small س in the first two i.e.

   a. وَيَبْضُطُ in Surah Baqarah and

   b. بَصْطَةً in Surah A'raaf س will be read, and in the third place.

   c. أَمْ هُمُ الْمُصَيْطِرُوْنَ in Surah <u>T</u>oor either a س or a ص could be read, and in the fourth place.

   d. بِمُصَيْطِرٍ in Surah Ghashiyah ص must be read.

QUESTIONS

1. What is the common and technical meaning of waqf?

2. How many types of Waqf are there?

3. Give a detail explanation, with examples of:

   a. Waqf-e-bil Iskaan

   b. Waqf-e-bil Ishmaam

   c. Waqf-e-bir Raum

4. Explain the terms:

   a. Waqf-e-Taam

   b. Waqf-e-Qabee<u>h</u>

5. Show the four places In which Saktah is wajib?

6. In which word is here Imalah?

7. Which word in Surah Hameem Sajdah is it necessary to make Tasheel in?

8. How should the word لَا تَأْمَنَّا in Surah Yusuf be read?

(EARNEST APPEAL)

An earnest appeal is made to the reader to please inform the publishers if any errors or shortcomings are discerned in this publication; for improving further editions of this publication. Your cooperation will be appreciated. Jazakallah.